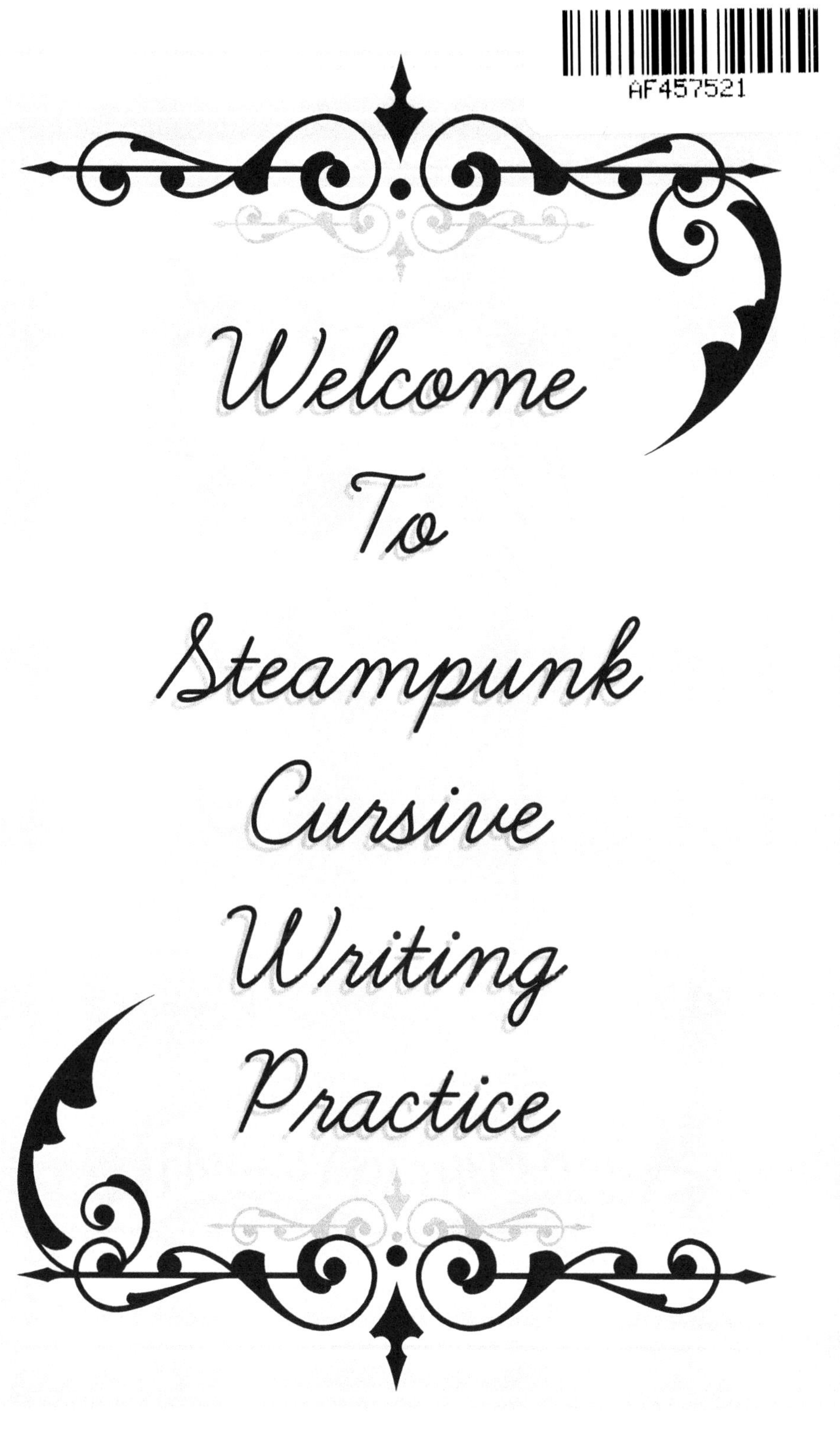
Welcome
To
Steampunk
Cursive
Writing
Practice

a, b, c

a a a a a a a

b b b b b b b

c c c c c c c

ab ab ab ab

bc bc bc bc bc

ac ac ac

abc abc abc

bac bac bac

cba cba cba

acb acb acb

cab cab cab

d, e, f

d d d d d d

e e e e e e e

f f f f f f f

de de de de

ef ef ef ef ef

df df df df

def def def

edf edf edf

fed fed fed

dfe dfe dfe

fde fde fde

g, h, i

h h h h h h h

g g g g g g g

i i i i i i i

gh gh gh gh

hi hi hi hi hi

gi gi gi gi gi

ghi ghi ghi

igh igh igh

hgi hgi hgi

ihg ihg ihg

gih gih gih

j, k, l

j j j j j j j

k k k k k k

l l l l l l l

jk jk jk jk jk

kl kl kl kl

jl jl jl jl jl

jkl jkl jkl

kjl kjl kjl

lkj lkj lkj

jlk jlk jlk

ljk ljk ljk

m, n, o

m m m m

n n n n n

o o o o o o

mn mn mn

no no no no

mo mo mo

mno mno

nmo nmo

onm onm

mon mon

omn omn

p, q, r

p p p p p p

q q q q q q

r r r r r r r

pq pq pq pq

pr pr pr pr

qr qr qr qr

pqr pqr pqr

qpr qpr qpr

rqp rqp rqp

prq prq prq

rpq rpq rpq

s, t, u

s s s s s s s s

t t t t t t t t

u u u u u u u

st st st st st

su su su su

tu tu tu tu

stu stu stu

tsu tsu tsu

uts uts uts

sut sut sut

ust ust ust

v, w, x

v v v v v v

w w w w w

x x x x x x

vw vw vw

vx vx vx vx

wx wx wx

vwx vwx vwx

wvx wvx wvx

xwv xwv xwv

vxw vxw vxw

xvw xvw xvw

x, y, z

x x x x x x

y y y y y y

z z z z z z z

xy xy xy xy

xz xz xz xz

yz yz yz

xyz xyz xyz

yxz yxz yxz

zyx zyx zyx

xzy xzy xzy

zxy zxy zxy

Numbers

1 1 1 1 1 1

2 2 2 2 2

3 3 3 3 3

4 4 4 4 4

5 5 5 5 5

6 6 6 6 6

7 7 7 7 7

8 8 8 8 8

9 9 9 9 9

0 0 0 0 0

1234567890

Artwork I painted onto an upcycled mirror

www.retrovandal.com

Short Words

Cat Cat

Dog Dog

Rat Rat

Owl Owl

Mice Mice

Bug Bug

Bird Bird

Fish Fish

Squid Squid

Pig Pig

Cow Cow

Short Words

Boat Boat

Ship Ship

Port Port

Sea Sea

Wave Wave

Tug Tug

Aft Aft

Bell Bell

Sail Sail

Rope Rope

Oar Oar

Short Words

Fire Fire

Gas Gas

Oil Oil

Can Can

Iron Iron

Air Air

Gold Gold

Tin Tin

Ore Ore

Lead Lead

Ash Ash

Artwork I created from upcycled objects & materials

www.retrovandal.com

Medium Words

Steam Steam

Engine Engine

Balloon Balloon

Airship Airship

Pipes Pipes

Piston Piston

Hinge Hinge

Screw Screw

Rivet Rivet

Bolted Bolted

Ornate Ornate

Medium Words
Smoke Smoke
Pressure Pressure
Noise Noise
Grind Grind
Oily Oily
Grease Grease
Dials Dials
Tubing Tubing
Output Output
Pivot Pivot
Wrench Wrench

Medium Words

Wood Wood

Leather Leather

Padded Padded

Corset Corset

Chains Chains

Studded Studded

Rivets Rivets

Twine Twine

Lacing Lacing

Ruffles Ruffles

Fabric Fabric

Artwork I created using air dry clay

www.retrovandal.com

Long Words

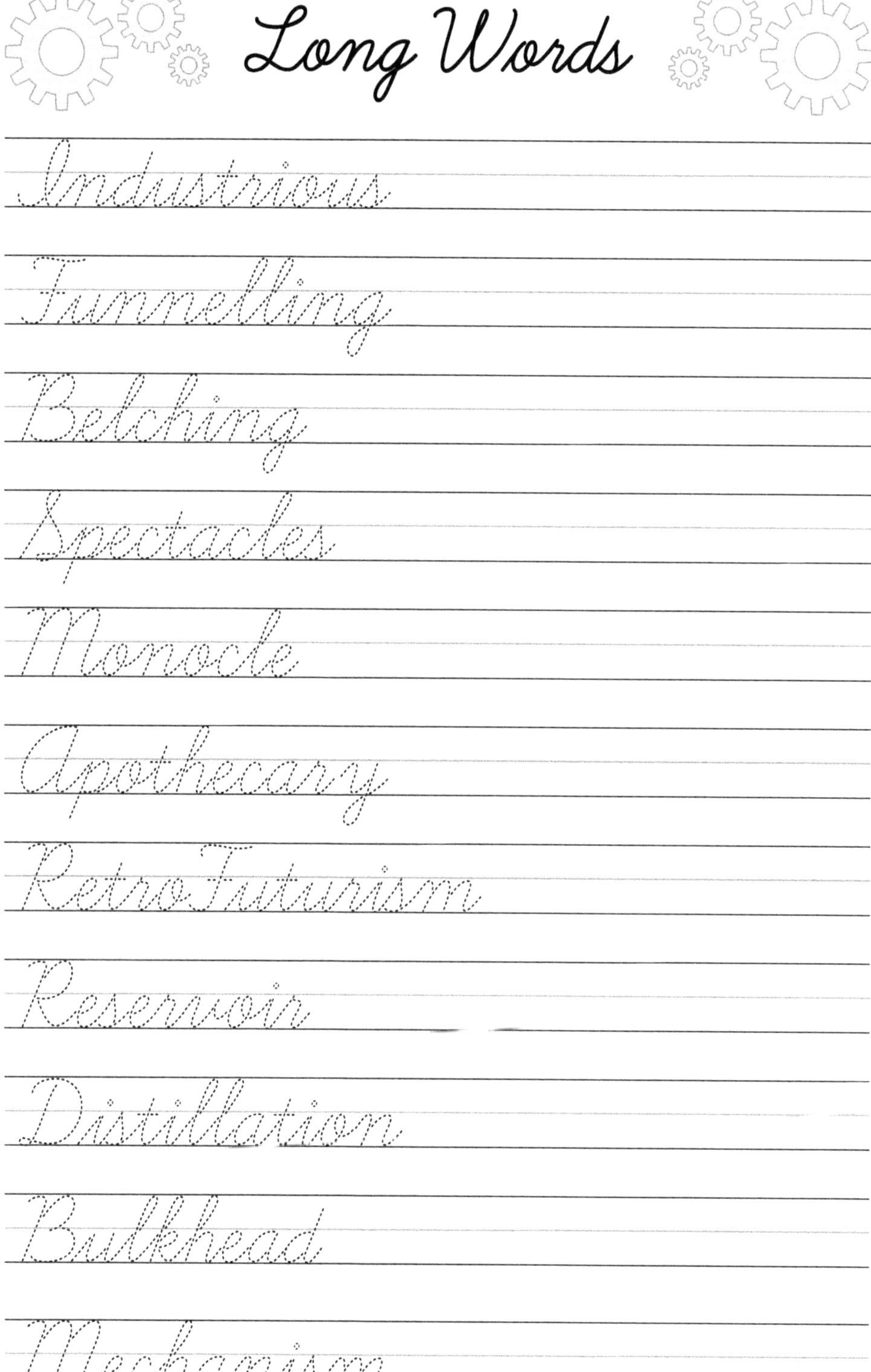

Industrious
Tunnelling
Belching
Spectacles
Monocle
Apothecary
Retro Futurism
Reservoir
Distillation
Bulkhead
Mechanism

Long Words

Phosphore

Clockwork

Observatory

Laboratory

Ornithopter

Aeronaut

Articulated

Combustion

Fulminated

Bombardier

Contraption

Long Words

Quicksilver
Corrosion
Crucible
Coruscating
Wanderlust
Incendiary
Whalebone
Horsehide
Gauntlet
Skulduggery
Cataclysmic

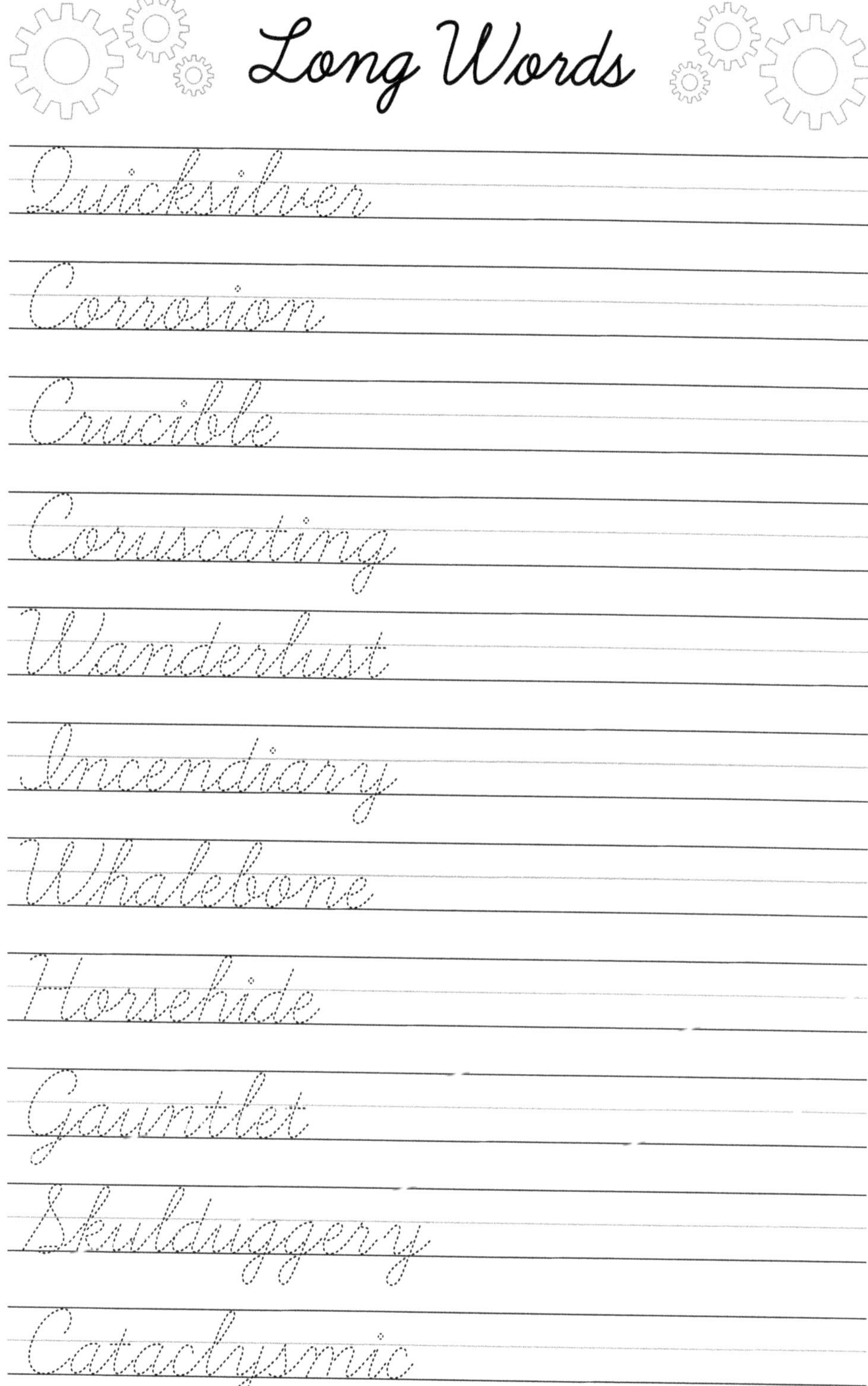

Artwork I created using upcycled junk objects

www.retrovandal.com

Phrases

Beware of the Journeyman

Smoke belching from the chimney

The cogs and gears were grinding

The pressure level was dangerous

Pistons were pumping frantically

The engine fired into life loudly

The air balloon was about to burst

The mechanism revealed a secret

His name was embossed in gold

Ornate patterns adorned the exterior

Baroque details surrounded the motif

Her gloves were from moleskin

Gouts of flame burst from within

Cuththroat Charley was loitering

Dastardly deeds were to transpire

Blackhearted by name and nature

The inspector glanced in my direction

A plume of smoke rose ominously

There was a rupture in the main pipe

She agreed to meet in her chamber

The aperture opened with a hiss

The distillation of the liquid began

A compass was what she needed

Contact the artificer to make another

He had to get to the apothecary fast

Wrenching the bolt off was easy

Fisticuffs was inevitable at this point

The inventor must have been insane

Phrases

The areodrome buzzed with activity

Heat from the furnace warmed us

His quilted jacket stopped the bullet

The reservoir was empty, what next?

Clothes supplied by the quartermaster

Drinks a plenty at the public house

The ironworks were in the distance

Phrases

Within the bell jar was a specimen

She was bronzing the exterior

The rivets are not going to hold

As we plummeted earthward

The side was riddled with bullet holes

Fire scorched his face as it opened

Smoke in her eyes blinded her

A barrage hit the ship immediately

Godspeed my child she whispered

Dials were showing signs of danger

Noxious fumes emitted from within

The lantern was lit, but helped little

Huge bellows began to fill it with air

He folded like a deflating concertina

Phrases

She brandished a firearm menacingly

A rupture in the pipe could be fatal

It was about to detonate so we ran

There was nothing genteel about it

The skipper shouted at the storm above

A boffin arrived to fix the machine

Urchins gathered around the body

Master & Mistress they ruled it all

The governor strode in with authority

Golden scrollwork adorned its body

His top hat was found on the floor

She rushed headlong into the fray

The lens needed cleaning very badly

Grease on his hands proved nothing

Phrases

Aftermath ash fell like snowflakes

The flint sparked and the gas ignited

He put on his monocle to inspect it

You would need a spyglass to read it

It came plummeting from the sky

I think a gasket has blown, mine

Circumnavigate the islands this time

Rising skyward it amazed us all

A look of wonderment on her face

It was airborne but not for long

Clockwork mechanism whirred to life

Gears and cogs ground to halt

By gaslight he could see the corpse

The dirigible sailed overhead silently

Phrases

Valves blew as the water boiled off

The armature fell off all by itself

He engraved her name on to it

Clockwork powered it was a miracle

Made out of iron it was very sturdy

He donned his goggles and rode off

The flywheel turned and up he went

Artwork I created using upcycled junk objects

www.retrovandal.com

Write down the events of yesterday - try to remember as many as you can - and write it in cursive

Make a list of all the people you know – friends & family – and write it in cursive!

Activities

Write down as many objects in the room as you can – and write it in cursive!

List all your favourite movies, books or games – and write it in cursive!

Write a letter to a loved one and express your feelings – and write it in cursive!

Write or copy a poem, song lyrics or phrases you like – and write it in cursive!

Make a list of every word you can think of relating to Steampunk – and write it in cursive!

Write a very short Steampunk story

– and write it in cursive!

Make a list of all the craziest inventions you can imagine
Combine several things into one - and write it in cursive!

Trapped in a runaway airship you must escape
Write down how you would do it – and write it in cursive!

Practice writing very long words – and write them in cursive!

Artwork I created inspired by Cthulhu
www.retrovandal.com

Artwork I created on a vintage brass plate
www.retrovandal.com

www.ingramcontent.com/pod-product-compliance
Ingram Content Group UK Ltd.
Pitfield, Milton Keynes, MK11 3LW, UK
UKHW021925190726
13853UKWH00002B/860

9 798464 292918